a false paradise

poems by Brian Rigg

MISFIT

ecw press

NATIONAL LIBRARY OF CANADA CATALOGUING IN PUBLICATION DATA

Rigg, Brian
A false paradise

Poems.
ISBN 1-55022-481-6

I. Title.

PS8583.I4192F34 2001 C811'.6 C2001-900813-9
PR9199.4.R54F34 2001

Edited by Michael Holmes / a misFit book
Cover and text design by Tania Craan
Cover art and author photo by Kevin Brewer
Layout by Mary Bowness

Printed by AGMV

Distributed in Canada by
General Distribution Services,
325 Humber College Blvd.,
Toronto, ON M9W 7C3

Published by ECW PRESS
2120 Queen Street East, Suite 200
Toronto, ON M4E 1E2
ecwpress.com

This book is set in Garamond.

PRINTED AND BOUND IN CANADA

The publication of *a false paradise* has been generously supported by the Canada Council, the Ontario Arts Council and the Government of Canada through the Book Publishing Industry Development Program. Canada

content

ACKNOWLEDGEMENTS

Some of these poems were first published in following journals: *Grain, paperplates, Windsor Review, Acta Victoriana, Da Juice!, The Harpweaver, Kola, Propaganda, Fireweed, Canadian Dimension, Backwater Review* and *Existere.* To the editors and publishers, my gratitude. Thanks also to the Parkdale Poetry Project, The Canadian Poetry Association and the Ma'ka team.

just these four babies, stories told by toads and *a fountain* were inspired by the artwork of Marlene Dumas. Green Island, in *blue window story,* is a small parish in Jamaica where I spent the first 7 years of my life. Needle was the name of one of my grandmother's favourite dogs. *night blossoms* is for Amir, Yorrick and Wayne, for all our crazy nights. *tiger lily* is for Ms. Tiger Lily, one of the fiercest drag queens on the local scene. The poem *entitled* speaks to those who are still suffering from the legacies of war. Innsmouth, in *strange passing,* is the name of a small, eerie coastal town in H.P. Lovecraft's short story "Shadow Out of Innsmouth." Tadzio, from Thomas Mann's *Death In Venice,* inspired a *Venetian fuge; the preacher's boy* is for the great James Baldwin. The epigraph is from Louise Bennett's "Writing Home."

This collection would not have been possible without the love, faith and support of my close friends Louise, Wayne, Sandra and Kevin. I would also like to thank Gary Hophan and Rhea Tregebov for their scholastic tutelage, and for imparting their love of the craft. Let me not forget Michael Holmes for his saintly patience, quiet persistence and editorial equity.

a false paradise is dedicated to Denise Kouroumalos,
who has been there from the beginning,
and for Raymond (Keebler) Siakkonen
who could not see it to the end.

Dear Mamma, how is tings
Ah hope yuh keeping well,
I have a good-time
Ah happy here so-tell,
I is not working now but ah
Jine in a labour set
An ah 'ope to keep awn striking
Tell some esteem jab ah get

— *Louise Bennett*

stories told by toads

the little gods

papa's moth flutters over our past
and with cold insect feet
grazes my father's heart,
then lands on mine.

my mother loves me a little less
every time she sees me.
I notice it in her probing eyes,
in the way she will sometimes say
"you have your father's chin."

I'm always trying to love her a little more,
ever since at five she left me
in the belly of a steel bird.

papa's moth is a history of pain,
whispers like shadows and dust
in the corners and hidden under the bed.

those little harms done,
quietly packaged and passed on from son to son,
never allowing us a bursting out
like snake skin caught on branches.

with only the permission of a small faith
in the little gods of loss, of insects and secrets,
our love was a suffocated love, drowned
in the depths of ether.

house of flies

Alex opens up his house of flies
and when we move through it
the scent of new wood
is thick in the air,
his family's presence
heavy in my throat.

the distance seems to grow
between us
with all the summers
he must have spent here

with dead cats in the barn
and a thousand images captured
by his mother's eyes —
placed in the album and colour-coded —

brown for barn life.

in the corners, he shows me
dead flies up-ended
and crisp under my feet,

in the bay windows and attic
an open mass grave, like old raisins
gathered and bathed
in pools of collected light.

with him in the rain and warmth
I'm walking wounded
past his mother's garden,

the tall brown sunflowers
dead, but still standing to salute.

stories told by toads

the moon pours down
off our backs in the hot sun
expanding —
a well-slung pebble
the membrane exploding

these are stories told by toads
of night-songs in green
slime and mud by the pool

beneath
long strings of black eyes
in clumps around reeds

flattened on the road

or lying on our backs
eyes bulging, limbs spread apart
an invitation to the knife

the question of dementia in certain house spiders

the spider finally shows itself
one night late in February —
I think it must have gone mad
          from a long winter
spent exiled in a cool crevice
somewhere in my room

because pushing it with a pen
only causes agitation,
the outcome
when paid close attention to
is small mandibles biting,
attempts to cocoon
          the ball-point end

retracting all eight brittle legs as if to
spring at the harsh blow of my breath
and its attacking origin, mouth

would normally kill it
          without hesitation
flattened under some scrap paper
impaled on a pin
or burned at the candle's fire

but who could deny it
a chance at
another year's stealthy
          mating

reincarnation

to come back as a poison arrow frog
so brightly red warding and deadly

bearing a quiet young or two on my
sticky back, to drop off in a pitcher plant
full of safe water

to feed on mosquito larvae
and the occasional infertile egg

or a butterfly
delicate in three life stories
having two coming outs

sucking only at pretty flower throats
flying everyday on strong winds
above everything below

the false paradise of such things

blue window story

.

beyond the blue window
        mama's white sheets hand-washed
                and sun-glimpsed in a gunmetal basin,
make us squint to stare.

blending in with clouds heavy and
cumulous, hanging suspended
in the early afternoon sky.

as a boy, jumping up to watch
my cousins teasing the dog,
                        ticks like swollen bullets
                    dotting needle's thin body.

..

                    mama calling me back down
        beside her to read Solomon's song,
or some other passage.
        but still yearning for up there,
                    the rhyming smack of
pink elastic rope kissing stone.

her mouth collapsed
        without dentures that are
                too painful for aged and tired gums.

intently she was always scrubbing
at clothes never quite clean —
clean calling out corrections with
one cocked eye shiftless
behind small lenses
round and cracked.

...
in late evenings
this Green Island stretches down
the road, over dense cane fields
and out-of-season mango trees
into a quiet cerulean sea.

so many uncles sitting on the veranda,
slapping down serious games of domino
into a smoky Craven A haze.
their too early rum-shouts
heard throughout the old house.

....
only my aunt Rose's head reaching to my chest,
hunched back
her growth stunted by a fear of milk
and so many days fighting
with our coarse knotty hair,
her one self
gutting sweet green peas on the back steps.

at night, June calls our kamikaze crabs
out of water holes and
down from dank hillside burrows,
                    their luminous shells
caught in moon glow
side-dancing off the road,
the smell of gutters running with fresh rain.

good hands

my father, who was of the earth,
would have liked to plant us
with good hands, he said,
"mamma brought me up like this
and I grew up strong."

Keron and I at these times
had meetings in the cupboard

plotting to put cockroaches
in his Sunday soup.

my mother, who was not hers,
was always in the other room
just where he wanted her,
she was not of the earth either —
his good hands were wasted on her.

my sister and I would always wait
for the summer to come

but when it did, she would find
those scars were still there
like old illegitimacies,
that feeling she would get
when close to him, or any man.

to aunt Cynthia

nine at night in Kingston
salt and sugar mixed with a little rum
on a plate beside the Bible

told her of the two old women
drawing back the curtains
saw the familiarity
of her feet and knew

then up to a face
darkened by the sickness

imagine in that house
the little man putting down
one piece of singing
said she never heard singing
since she left the island

the wake lasted all week
she all the time in the kitchen
over a hot stove, putting
out goat-head soup for everyone

and how she even forgot
to buy the clothes
for burying her sister in

leaving the airport
my mother in the car tells me
she wished I was there, by her side

crab season

the still warm bread
cut into rough slices and
eaten with onion-fried fish

crickets calling in the dusk

this I'm told, is crab season
at the roadside,
zinc-hooded shanties
struggle for supremacy

driving to the market
a hot breeze blowing
into the van
            with the after-images
of black boys in khaki suits
walking home from school

plays well with other children

after birth he is trademarked, registered
in witness of this day, Alicia and Roy
on Thursday, at 6:28 a.m., think they love him.

sticky colour-coded stars given for cat. bat. sat.
sitting outside Mr. Whitehorn's office,
almost every day a fight over phonetics,
his right to own language.

his father would send him mandalas
from prison, prayers etched in pencil,
his own vision of Inuit cathedrals
flourishing in the north.

at 5, a boat: brown swirls collapsing in
on themselves and running off the page;
remembers this mess and tries to be now, pure —
still no colour yet for sky.

landing on ESL steps with a long black umbrella
procured for a daily beating down of Babel's words,
there are no records of this, or reports cards that read:
plays well with other children.

strange passing

.

in Ottawa the police look at you
like a shadow out of Innsmouth,
fishy eyes alien to the need for just cause —

a drive-by feels as if you're doing it,
this random act of violence is a
casual stray glance entering the base
of your skull and exiting
just above your left eye.

..

cycling across the Champlain Bridge
one rogue web falls, embraces brow and
with a quiet persistence wraps itself around my ears
holds on tightly for the entire strange passing.

all there seems left is a
hate of bridges, especially at night,
with water under them, how this whole place
seems to be bordered by these connections.

...

the street corners angle
like the awkward bony elbows
of children raised in a place where
it is good to raise children.

heads pivot reluctantly on resistant necks,
with considerably less range
than other necks in other cities, 45 degrees,
or must be directly confronted before being
graced with a furtive and suspicious stare.

....

if cities dream, then this one for a deeper
more extensive root system than it has been given —
an end to the harsh grinding of stone, the slow
winding course of perpetual construction.

raspberries

— for Denise

making our way
cautiously through thorns
the patches lined along
                              the side

Denise
with her mouth full
cheeks smeared deep red

hands cupped,
and olive-tanned
in the sun

                    the back of her legs
disappearing further
into the bush
we discuss the sweet ones
and how they would be good
with cream

in dark June

— for Ray (June 12, 1973 to June 14, 1996)

seeing the sign on my way to work,
"hockey players needed!"
like a cold stone fist, reminds me of you.
on this morning your death is close again.

a picture at nine, all long legs wrapped in foam,
white-blond hair and big hands
bulging eyes behind those thick lenses,
frightened-looking and partly playing that game
because everyone else wanted you to.

dead you are dead and lying cold,
surrounded by a deep red space
at the viewing, and one more time knowing
that I must touch your skin — that your death is
so organized and already vague.

how you loved Fridays; the song,
our game, the true passion time
when we all played together;

i'm hard against the night you died,
that wicked bullet weaving its way into your chest
minutes after I talked to you.

in dark June it was graceless,
your life unraveled some time in the night
you died alone.

atrophy

watching together these two large cats
making spinster love on the sill
licking each other in a light rain,

in the beginning was
a feigned interest in thirsty plants
by the window, just to be near you.

there is a certain kind of atrophy
in staying in the kitchen, paying
too close attention to grease stains.

what he wouldn't understand
is that I like the shape his mouth makes
when it says "you,"

is how to watch my cough floating
in water, smile when you think it's a
funny man-o-war in green.

instead I'm always watching him
leave, to go out into the under
where the weather is waiting.

ghetto palm

her life with him must have been
the ghetto palm growing
in a concrete room

grey light sliced into rays
coming down from barred windows
placed high out of reach
without prayer or cement psalm

her ear cotton-stuffed
honey smeared on eyelids
smooth rocks slipped
down her throat
a suppression of all these senses

left to smile in the depths of sorrow
stoic at the height of joy
travel blind and only by night

because submission is a
monkey's grin, all teeth and fear, this
is what she must have shown to him

that you should swallow it all down
with the no colour of rain
and sunless days

take it with the after-storm glow
and perfectly neutral air

Carmen sinks beneath the weighty sea,
moves amongst the swirling masses
of mute fish
silent in the dark bottom

because she was led to believe that
discord is a high cracked note
left bleeding in the air

my mother in my arms doesn't know she
smells like too many years of hard work,
cooking oil and provisions from the market

all the spindly roots of dusty yams
lying in the creases of her tired smile

entitled

this is a village of crutches and bloody stumps,
an industry of artificial legs, some place
where ghost limbs flicker out in the bush.

long after wars end
flies roam over brown-stained gauze
and other flies, jockey for position and puss.

the first explosion lifts the land mine
to a height of $3^{1}/2$ feet,
the second, leaves few lame children.

for just pennies, a pound of flesh,
splinters of bone and shrapnel ripped
through the legs, backed by fire.

military reason; a dead soldier is
sometimes buried, but usually passed over,
the crippled lower morale, drain resources.

Africville

but when I journeyed back to
that place of dark skins, I did not see flowers,
I was told flowers bloomed brighter here,
just as the sun.

and I could remember the days
when light danced off these waters
and we would gather up the children
and take them to the seaside.

this was the place where
pipes carried the white man's waste
to our shores and we were glad to
have their dumpsites at our doorsteps.

this was when a family got lead poisoning
from burning car batteries for heat,
and I said, "God, what is this place?"

this was our home they told me, we were
never closer then, now, only to a sense of it.

when they came to take us away, it was
with the surprise that Miss Hatty's house was
no longer there. "I'm so old, it really doesn't
matter to me, it's the children I worry about."

it would be the young boy who woke up
one morning and asked,
"Mom, where did the church go?"

there was no better place than this place
by the sea, away from their cold cities,
we lived in houses each one a different colour

I remember my father lifting me up to
smell a tall flower   a red one.

ubengi

don't comb your hair so natural,
you'll look like a man
don't wear so much beads,
you'll look like a ubengi
and don't wear so much red,
your skin is too black.

now that you're thirty, thinking back
on all those don'ts, like dead ends,
nerves and cells in your body —
you liked the colour red.

now all the damage has been done,
botched surgery on your self-esteem,
besides, she's your mother.

but the colour red is still bad
blood in your mouth and
when next to your skin.

and suddenly those don'ts
have come back to haunt you,
like heirlooms
you're passing them down
to your children.

don't wear so much gold,
it makes you look cheap, and
why don't you take those dreads

out of your head
you'll never get a job and
don't always sound so political,
men don't want to hear that.

now that you're old
you wonder why your daughter
doesn't come to visit you more often.

now that you're thirty thinking back
on all those don'ts
you begin to wonder, what was a ubengi
and was it such a bad thing?

the preacher's boy

preacher man's son
running on old cracked concrete,
on either side, corn fields
stretching out the day

down dirt road to the church
the little black girls hanging off
their mama's freshly pressed Sunday dress

inside so hot, makes most female
hands wave lazy fans,
every man with a handkerchief,
his father's voice rising above,
sinking deep into exposed wood
strong and rich, beside his mother

it is black-eyed peas, fresh chicken,
the droplets of collected water
on his mother's best pitcher, on

time seems plenty for hard days
of clansmen and marches,
the stinging bite of water hose
and sharp teeth of police dogs,
the coming birth of his new faith

this woman

this woman kneels by
the riverside, washing clothes
white on stone

washing away the day's sorrows
before going home

the life of this woman is in the fields
her hands brown
with dried and rich soil
back bent over but always under
the hot sun

in the distance the church
sacred bone of earth thrust
against day-blue sky

she can hear now
Sunday's lovely service, her sisters
tilling long brown rows of pews
working there too

on rare early mornings she meets
the man she jumped broom with

seeing his daughter for the first time
is glad he came that winding way

the life of this woman is life still
for many, still as the ground
beneath her feet

slow as the cycles all around her
the flow of her menses

mike

mike listens and tries to interrupt
the confines of his pheno-type,
what he hears now
is the sound rot makes, a de-composition,
the way my eyes feel in their sockets.

sees this house as numbers
that must add up to the stomping of feet,
math which equals the swinging
of arms above the head.

he's able tear it down,
this space where we go to have faith.
but right now he has the sound for
that feeling we couldn't put words to
earlier,

the kind of darkness that would
blacken the mouth to speak it, a hunger.
he holds it at the tips of his fingers,
touches the distances around it.

on the way home
a tire going flat reminds me of that sound,
how timid he is when circling
the goodness of his art, its bump.

displaced

the mime's art, you say,
is to creep
silently through the mouth —
and that's how you got that scar
at the tip of your head?

or maybe from a ball
on the playground

those ghoulish puppets
hanging still
              above the oval mirror
all bulbous and knobby-kneed

that one who is like Kali
with her arms wide open
whispers, "I wish them
all dead and under my feet"

after my scissors,
his dark hair fallen
all around us
seems to portend
something on Tuesday
like tea leaves and my leaving

in the corner of my room,
a new plant, pleomele
              (dracaena reflexa)

displaced,
the song of Jamaica
waits patiently for
morning's pale fingers

the false paradise of such things

from lake to land, a wall of green spruce
in between
I would hope to see a *Dani* girl
bridal in a skirt woven to her hips

arms rounding in tree-rat fur and a Bird of Paradise
feather headdress

a procession of grey hog's flesh ready for inspection
by the local *Wiscun* of Plevena Ontario,

me the groom searching in a bright yellow paddleboat
hunting still for dowry

by a shallow black water
with hook, line and the heavy weights of dream

preying upon the stupidity of fish —
the false paradise of such things

poems for Oleg

to Montreal in his car
Oleg sings a song in Spanish
given to him by a
former Mexican girlfriend,
taken by his eyes I bet

because it was not given
to him by me
I ask him to sing another song,
maybe one in Russian this time

in the kitchen Oleg is swaying,
his back arched over the wok
the space he makes is this:

a one-room place
        in Andean relief,
the Bossa Nova rhythms beating
        softly in the background

every day we enter into it,
the smell of tofu,
        spiced garlic with curry paste
on his futon where i'm sitting,
        i let it all move into me

on the table beside me
a small basket woven in
dark brown straw

holds three tangerines
in different shades of
orange and mottled green

across its polished surface
careful clippings of old recipes

forgetting me on the couch
Oleg gently leans over
his fragile mother, carefully picks
up the ones she wants as directed by

nerve shot hands
her fingers curling into wrinkled
pincers, looks over at me and smiles

sometimes I am afraid
to ask him for anything more

Oleg mutilates the cheese
with a long knife, slicing
the thin pieces off
a pockmarked wedge

like leaves falling
in a fan shape on
the small wooden cutting board

chewing each one with
some Russian-made sausage
and an ease ready-made

always forgets the lateness
of the hour
ignores my warning of
a sick stomach

night blossoms

tiger lily

tonight tiger lily will pop an e
        let melt under tongue 2 hits
                and when done
        putting on her face
smoke a fat one
to slow it all down

        her dress will be coded
stop-traffic yellow
there will be
a silver star
        on the front
                and under that
will be the word fucker

she will be a STARFUCKER

she will race to the white ball
faster than
her mind can catch up

at 10:45 am
        Sunday
she will drop down dead
tired

her hair will be her own
no wigs
for this real queen

and when she slaps
those black lace fans
on tight bright thighs
snaps them open
and poses
one plucked eyebrow
raised
you will know who she is

one of the last
to keep up this house
the vengeance
the fierceness
knows which school
she belongs to

and when tiger lily runways over
to that platform
boiled rice tits
cutting a path
through the fleshy crowd
no one will dare
because fame is cheap here

grey gardens

in these gray gardens only the fossil star, (let's)
watch as mother's scalpel
fingers slice up his many different selves.
up in the attic, a sea of leaves,

raccoons feeding on her Wonder Bread
nibble at long hands, a widowed baby Jane
he is already scratching at corners.

never knowing the day he
got stuck in the middle of remaking memories,
fighting for them and when next to blame.

now whispers resentments
from the other rooms and softly, softly,
he hums a soothing threat,

we alight on roads already taken,
careful not to set traps, reel in undertones
smooth over long silences, we leave no stains.

her things always have something to say here:
flowers, plastic and imitation gold,
painted and porcelain ladies and gentlemen

welcome me with accusations of never coming home.
the imprecision of our voices suggest
a guessing at where we lost words for love,

speak carefully around potted aloe vera and
creeping fern, we hold an easy question at knifepoint.

night blossoms

lipstick smeared like blood down
our chins, white bone
thrust needles through
fish nets raking over exposed spine.
heard in the lonely calm in
punctuated clicks of
bullet-studded heels making
deep furrows
around gunmetal corners,
the border between

second and third eye.
possessing a skin used only
for accent, additives
of dashing masala backdrops,
stripped wallpaper relevant for
highlighting certain
classes of other less distinct colour,
smudged pastels,
electric copper hues,
all of ill-strewn fairy vomitus,

corporate sygils etched into every corridor,
into every passing day,

we entered into pastel nightmares.

cut our tongues on exposed nerves,
sold asses from high
plush red leather stools,
                    fell from grace in
out-of-order washroom stalls.

we walked these dead roads where
                hope ran down gutters, varicosed.
sullen moths flew up from our throats,

        we saw the night's end
                    in the old eyes of men,
divined it in the street's concrete entrails.

waiting for meaning

it used to be I lied on my back
waiting for meaning
in a hotel, already paid for

on hard beds and

in the back of car seats
sometimes a sheet spread
to contain the mess.

sometimes it's easier
on my hands and knees
the waiting

in a church

inside soft coffins
my legs dangling from the sides —
stained glass
above and all around.

black flower

.

she is so deep in make-up, black mod and eyes feline
a cat's dark lips pushing at 16, an egg hard
boiled somewhere on the turf of Viki's town

pushing deeper still into hot self-induced
hey girl, you are just one black flower.

child woman child you have to
live on lettuce leaves, all your life pleasing
these lolitas with golden locks casting
spiral shadows at your feet

tell me, what are your choices? cocaine or
crack-kitsch, that corner of Bleeker and Carlton
your own private runway

those stray dogs with blue/green reflective
lenses privy to your patented brand
of street glamour strut.

..

oh mama I'm so lost, never
coming home — my eyes full as puffer fish,

mama the boys in the back are still stinging
my neck with dick, arrested me sometime after
thirteen, but in that all women's house it was like family.

they had me play games of tea bagging in the park.
moon trapping and dress-up were good substitutes
for sun block and ejaculate.

...

in this dreaming I would be Mamy Fisher;
have outrageous parties for my
2 dozen-some-odd-dogs, or

I could be a palm bitch in technicolor
those paparazzi cameras become clits
after all that evil Jim Beam.

gonna go down south one by one
day gonna find myself out
somewhere deep in folds of heat —
she will be singing this justice, waiting

for me to crawl back into the ovum, wink out
at tuning fork chop-sticks
tapping away at ultrasonic beats
to choose a new birth sound, bust a style 9.

neon sons

we return again to these same pools,
gathering under neon suns and
as one primordial cell, we twitch

in unison, breathe in these same streets
with unfinished lungs
hop to the crocus of night
          ply on our wicked goods.

over time we become bitter by default
grow strange, even to our selves.

night calls us and we secretly listen,
go underground, shape our fears
                    into flightless birds and run.

wedding day

clocked at a slow and graceful arc
at speeds of over thirty years —
an artefact of the body,
her fleshy dowry, she
is letting it fly

her only gift is bashful
pink as soft light on rose
a full bloom in view
of new white sheets

she will kick it down
to the wary curves
satin-mutilated stems
bound tightly

still, a wedding dress
with hands holding a mountain
of petals free-falling
bouquets thrusting from
pelvises scrubbed
into a jagged bruise for this day only

dropping it like a hot stone
she embraces cool church steps,
goes down willingly, to be quickly
ripped apart by eager maiden fingers

with the auditors

no more Ms. Flowers, joy and sin
never took account of what
lay before her and within
cut down to one too many
dimensions,
a slice of infinite grey fruit
tucked between sheet and skin.

if Paris was burning

when Sherlock walked in
you knew he was there
heads turned to him
like a compass to north

his dark frame seemed
to stretch to the hard lights above
throbbed to the heavy beat

eyes heavy too with
the sultry mood of
dry ice and dreams

and when he hugged you
arms wrapped around
your body in coils pulling
you up and up to him

Sherlock was too damn bad

when he moved
onto the dance floor
it was cool quicksilver
to cut the crowd
in freeze-frame poses
to make your heart

flounder
to stumble and fall
into his rhythm-smooth steps

too bad Sherlock felt
he had to put on a dress
more and more
never dancing anymore
because he couldn't even
walk in those heels

too bad only the extension
of his hands for a greeting
only the kiss kiss
on a cheek
with painted red lips
and sharp nails
cutting into your skin

too damn bad
all Sherlock could say was
girl
only if Paris was burning
would I be there!

the division of pansies

in throwing you down the stairs we
heard the sound of tapping, we stumbled
in late knowing
        this was just a punk pushing at
four letter word therapies into a rhythmless naming,
                splicing a chalk circle of pansies
                        massive in constant social mitosis

just take a pulse no /rage /just stumble again
so much more I have in my little toes
even if you tell me they could kick my ass easily

        and do you believe the floor has
                jilted, left me swaying to the burn
        of your voice in some odd turn; here is some advice: listen,
        for hot splinters of noises in the blood
the inconsistent skelter of a hollow beat

Snow White in the wrong story

in the wrong story
trapped

between one glass box
and any other

her eyes opening
to hushed whispers

the people looking in
at you
speaking in silence

their mouths Os
dark holes
and eyes to avoid

you push with
alien hands and feet
to the sides and up

the screams you make
sound-proofed

in the wrong story
she never gets away

safely

never out

trace

trace

trace all these days I have been working on you and think
when it is finished you will surprise me with
a birth of asymmetry.
with inquisitive fingers I will touch the angles of your feet
and somehow know how to write them. even blind I will listen for
the constant warble in your heated throat.

the cynical transitions between states,
like blossoming clouds of apricot, is the chemistry of
windblown iron turning its attention homeward again.
no more important than these are my eyes, to see us
growing into every stroke of your hand,

the structure of leaves, the glassy overtures of snow drifts
all this time rushing through our uneven limbs. swirling around
the tense edges of this sudden life where we contend
and attempt to pattern last winter's ice storm.

there always, the danger in understanding branches angled
at 45 degrees, gained in trust, the season's little mutilations,
the uneasy truce of flayed bark and birch poised within
the stillness of coming rain.

a new edition is in everyday, like the unobserved dispensation
of our controlled dreaming. it's a little give, measured out in time
with a sometimes savage crash and bang. yes,
those beats are complicated too, provoking the silence
after thunder.

a Venetian fugue

I am the gentle lift of a mouth in white
and navy blue — horizontal and striped, a breeze
                                        from the Adriatic Sea.
dirty sand easing into blond, strawberry lips
eating strawberries.

                              there is a phantom on the beach
            yelling your name
to come in and be warm,
dance barefoot with long black frocks
                              shelter under creamed umbrellas
touch the sudden blush of cheek, again.

raise the suspicion of genteel Donnas
covered in mosquito-net shawls —
            breathe deeply in, just beneath the waves.
                              smile when no one is looking,
leave this place in a strangled hush.

a fountain

the little girl
with smooth black
hair cut short
just above the ears

skipping
on the sidewalk

her back
from above
grey and glistening
maybe
          already
dead

this is the position
he holds her in

late at night

bending over
her nakedness

a fountain

still new words waiting to be said, like the pear blossoms

far from reach of land
dragon kite flying, its
wings painted so fiercely,
terrible and beautiful.
its tail, a broken string,
can no longer be tethered to
this child's hand, leaving
him in this sudden wind.
neither of them asking
for such freedom.

just these four babies

the baby that knows
too much
sits propped up by a pillow,
eyes all black

not quite self-sufficient.

a somber little mouth —
sad almost.

a blue-eyed baby
smiling,
pink tongue poking over
a bruised mouth.

all must have good memories.

the little girl, too young
for red lips,
that dark brown one, sold
against his will.

third life

they would come secretly to him
from the outside
with those little inhuman details
the fees sometimes found
within the formal remains
of bodies left behind

tonight sat lotus style
looking over: copper rimmed glasses
eviscerated atomic pacemaker
and one blue marble eye

he liked to chew
on the crust of stale bread
watch the fire struggle to hold form
hypnotized in its glow
the persistent grinding of teeth

would observe the exposed bone
crack
burst open
bleed and bubble
its tender marrow

hoped that someone would drop
off a young male
fragile, bird-chested, contemplated
prayed for such things

evening caught him and the fire
dim and out of euphoric tongue

..

looked once above his circle
of cooling stone to see
distant smoke curling into hands
above the city
many small hands grasping
at individual stars
saw in between them

the red circle burn on a lover's
guilty neck, a child's coelacanthic spine

the widow's sleeping breath
a million heavy
murderous pillows, weighted ankles

the knowing stones thrown at her buried head

the strange ways of implants
more and more these days
like secret messengers of ending

prosthesis and pins
customised and slipped
just under our unsuspecting skins

sometimes thought he heard

their last signalled whispers
fire along cranial faultlines

in the splitting of femur
the meddling smoke of aged tobacco

...
then something mercurial and out
of every opening poured
an electronic ticking
into a slow and destined fall

with a certainty that introduced him
when his head said to cobbled floor

"how many long hours later until we are still
tasting it in the exhaust of singed hair, this
the under-tongue oily residue of rigor?"

then will there come that prickling
strange and burning at the throat?
some great and microscopic roaming
out amongst us, out into the world

first locked on target, designed
then manufactured
class-based, sex-based
biological
terrorism comes to mind

....

he saved sanitary masks for
                    the horrid visits of business
                    always and the curious

                    never more wore gloves
            but still touched with care
the set fullness of cold lip, smooth
hands unflinching

always allowed for the intimacy of dermal contact

kissed into story, the final departure
was somehow immune